# Natural Disasters

# Tornadoes

### by
### Jean Allen

**Consultant:**
Stephen J. Colucci
Associate Professor of Atmospheric Sciences
Cornell University

CAPSTONE BOOKS
an imprint of Capstone Press
Mankato, Minnesota

Capstone Books are published by Capstone Press
151 Good Counsel Drive, P.O. Box 669, Mankato, Minnesota 56002
http://www.capstone-press.com

*Library of Congress Cataloging-in-Publication Data*
Allen, Jean, 1964-
    Tornadoes/by Jean Allen.
    p. cm.—(Natural disasters)
    Includes bibliographical references and index.
    Summary: Describes how and why tornadoes happen, the damage they can cause,
and some of the most destructive tornadoes of the past.
    ISBN 0-7368-0588-5
    1. Tornadoes—Juvenile literature. [1. Tornadoes.] I. Title. II. Natural disasters
(Capstone Press)

QC955.2 .A45  2001
551.55'3—dc21                                                    00-021319

**Editorial Credits**
Connie R. Colwell, editor; Timothy Halldin, cover designer and illustrator;
    Kia Bielke, illustrator; Heidi Schoof and Kimberly Danger, photo researchers

**Photo Credits**
FPG International LLC, 15; FPG International LLC/Telegraph Colour Library, 6
Gary Braasch Photography, 12
Historical Society of Greene County, Xenia, Ohio, 32
Index Stock Imagery, 10
International Stock/Warren Faidley, cover, 4, 8, 22, 34
James L. Shaffer/SHAFFER PHOTOGRAPHY, 28
Reuters/Sue Ogrocki/Archive Photos, 36
State Historical Society of Missouri, Columbia, 30
Unicorn Stock Photos/Jim Fly, 20; Jean Higgins, 26, 41; Aneal Vohra, 38
Visuals Unlimited/Rick Poley, 16

1  2  3  4  5  6  06  05 04  03  02  01

# Table of Contents

# Chapter 1

# Tornadoes

On a spring day in 1951, Roy Hall and his family were outside their home in McKinney, Texas. The weather was warm and humid. Hall noticed black clouds developing in the sky. White clouds from the south began to move toward the dark clouds. The Hall family knew a storm was approaching.

Hall's wife gathered the children and went inside. But Hall stayed outside. He watched as circles of clouds appeared in the sky. Green-colored rain fell from the clouds.

The sky above Hall grew dark. Lightning flashed and baseball-sized hail began to strike the house. Hall heard a rumble in the distance. The sound grew louder and louder.

**In 1951, a tornado hit the Hall home in McKinney, Texas.** ◁

Tornadoes are the most violent windstorms.

Hall ran inside. He yelled for his family to hide under a bed in the back of the house.

Suddenly, the noise and lightning stopped. The walls of the house began to shake. Hall watched as the wind threw objects in the air above him.

The house moved suddenly. Hall was thrown across the room. He looked up to see part of the roof missing. The storm had ripped his house off its foundation and thrown it into some nearby trees.

Hall looked through the hole in the roof and straight up into the storm. The storm looked like a huge pipe swaying back and forth. Its inner walls were lined with rings. Hall saw a bright cloud high above him at the top of the pipe. A strange blue light surrounded the house.

The light then disappeared. The darkness of the thunderstorm returned. Blowing debris knocked at the walls of the house. Suddenly, the storm was over. Daylight returned.

That day, the storm killed 100 people across Texas. But Hall and his family were lucky. They survived. Hall became one of the few people to see the inside of a tornado and survive.

## Tornadoes

Tornadoes are the most violent windstorms. People have compared tornadoes to wrecking

**A tornado has the power to destroy everything in its path.**

balls, bombs, and war combat zones. A tornado has the power to destroy everything in its path.

Tornadoes can occur in almost every part of the world. The polar regions are the only areas that do not have tornadoes. The United States experiences more tornadoes than any other country. About 1,000 tornadoes strike the United States each year.

The strong spiraling winds of a tornado can do amazing things. Winds from tornadoes may be greater than 300 miles (480 kilometers) per hour. These winds can throw cars through the air. They can peel the bark off trees. They can destroy one house and leave the next untouched. Tornadoes are among the most frightening and fascinating of all storms.

# Chapter 2

# Why Tornadoes Happen

Tornadoes are caused by natural changes in the weather. Certain weather conditions must exist for tornadoes to occur.

## Air Pressure

The atmosphere is a layer of air that surrounds the Earth. The atmosphere has weight. This weight on a surface is called air pressure.

Air pressure constantly changes. The air's temperature causes these changes. The sun warms air near the Earth. This air spreads out. Warm air is less dense than cool air. Warm air rises. Cool air compresses. This causes air to clump together and sink.

The atmosphere is a layer of air that surrounds the Earth.

▷ **Cumulus clouds are fluffy and white.**

A thin layer of air separates the warm air from the cool air. This layer is called a capping inversion. The warm air stays trapped beneath the capping inversion. The cool air stays above the capping inversion.

The sun continues to warm the Earth throughout the day. The warm air trapped below the capping inversion absorbs this warmth. The air then becomes even warmer. The warm air also absorbs moisture that rises from water on the Earth. This process is called evaporation.

The capping inversion sometimes breaks down. The warm air then bursts upward. This burst of warm air begins to cool as it travels up through the atmosphere. The warm air then condenses. The moisture that was absorbed into the warm air is squeezed out. The moisture settles on bits of dust in the atmosphere to form clouds. The moisture falls as rain when the clouds become too heavy.

## Thunderstorms and Tornadoes

Moisture first forms into cumulus clouds. These clouds are fluffy and white. The condensation process gives off heat. The heat causes the air inside the cumulus clouds to become warm and rise even higher.

Hot and humid weather conditions can cause cumulus clouds to become cumulonimbus clouds. Cumulonimbus clouds are dark and tall. Some of these clouds reach heights of 10 miles (16 kilometers). They can produce rain, thunder, lightning, winds, and hail. Cumulonimbus clouds sometimes are called thunderheads.

## Tornado Formation

Updrafts and downdrafts occur during a thunderstorm. Changing winds above a thunderstorm can cause the rising warm air to become a strong updraft. This flow of warm air works like a vacuum cleaner. Updrafts suck up more air from the ground. Downdrafts also form during thunderstorms. The warm air cools as it rises and then flows back down toward the ground.

One updraft and downdraft pair is called a cell. Many cells may form during a thunderstorm. All the cells in a storm sometimes work together. As this process happens, more air is sucked into the updraft. The updraft then becomes stronger and may begin to spin or rotate if the wind changes direction. This spinning group of cells is called a tornado.

**Cumulonimbus clouds produce rainstorms.**

## Where and When Tornadoes Occur

Tornadoes can occur almost anywhere if
weather conditions are right. But 90 percent of
all tornadoes occur in the United States. Every
state has experienced at least one tornado in
its history.

About 90 percent of tornadoes in the United
States occur in an area called Tornado Alley.
This region extends north from central Texas
through central Oklahoma, Kansas, and

Nebraska. Tornado Alley also includes parts of
Iowa and Missouri.

Two types of air affect weather patterns
in the Tornado Alley region. Warm, moist air
blows north from the Gulf of Mexico. Cold
air blows south from Canada. Thunderstorms
and tornadoes are more likely to form when
these two air masses meet.

Tornadoes can occur any time the weather
conditions are right. Most tornadoes form in
April, May, or June. The most common time
for tornadoes to strike is between 3 p.m. and
9 p.m. The ground and atmosphere are
warmest at these times. This warmth provides
storm systems with energy.

## Related Storms

Other types of storms share common features
with tornadoes. Like tornadoes, hurricanes
consist of strong winds whirling around an

**Tornadoes that occur over warm water are called
waterspouts.**

area of low air pressure. But hurricanes are much larger than tornadoes. A hurricane is similar to many thunderstorms combined into one giant storm. Hurricanes can be as large as 600 miles (966 kilometers) wide. They can last for several days or weeks.

Hurricanes usually form over warm tropical water. Warm, moist air causes these storms. Hurricanes weaken and break apart when they travel over land or cool water. In these conditions, hurricanes may produce tornadoes.

Tornadoes that occur over warm water are called waterspouts. Waterspouts are most common along the Gulf Coast. Waterspouts usually are less destructive than other tornadoes. They move slowly and may last for 10 minutes. These storms can be dangerous to boaters. About 100 waterspouts occur each month over the shallow coastal waters of the Florida Keys.

Dust devils occur in the desert. These storms are not considered tornadoes because they form in clear skies. Dust devils occur when a layer of air near the ground gets very hot. The mass of air breaks apart and bursts upward. Light winds spin this air mass. The storm then picks up sand and dirt.

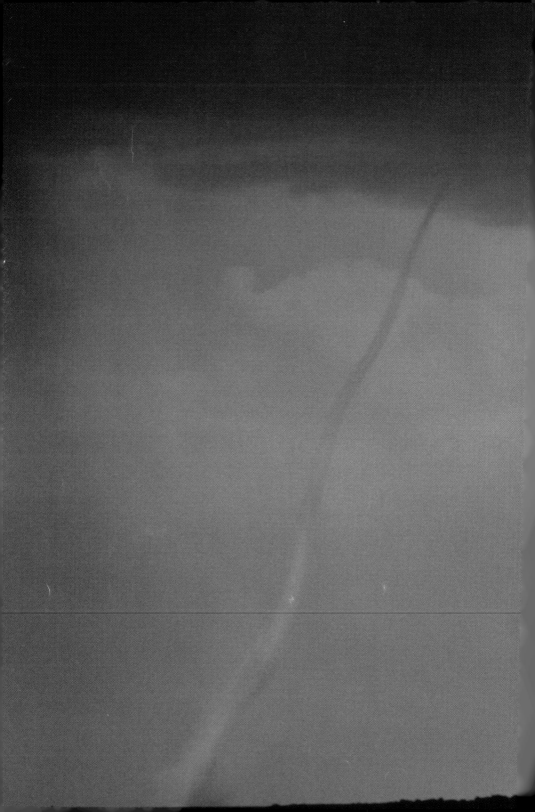

# Chapter 3

# The Power of a Tornado

All tornadoes are different. Tornadoes have different sizes, speeds, and life spans. A life span is the length of time that a tornado lasts.

## Tornado Sizes

A tornado's size is not related to its strength. Large tornadoes can be powerful or weak. Small tornadoes also can be powerful or weak.

A tornado's size also can vary during its life span. Tornadoes may be as small as 15 yards (14 meters) wide when they form. They can grow as large as 500 yards (457 meters) wide when they reach full strength. Tornadoes may shrink when they are in their last stages of life.

All tornadoes are different.

Most tornadoes last less than 15 minutes.

### Tornado Speeds

Most tornadoes rotate at speeds of 115 to 150 miles (185 to 241 kilometers) per hour. Severe tornadoes can reach speeds greater than 250 miles (400 kilometers) per hour. Most scientists agree that the top speed a tornado can reach is about 300 miles (480 kilometers) per hour.

Tornadoes also move across the ground as they rotate. Some tornadoes travel as slow as 5 miles (8 kilometers) per hour. Others travel as fast as 70 miles (113 kilometers) per hour. Most tornadoes travel at speeds of 10 to 20 miles (16 to 32 kilometers) per hour.

The rate at which tornadoes travel often determines their path of destruction. The damage path of a typical tornado might be 1 to 2 miles (1.6 to 3.2 kilometers) long and about 50 yards (45 meters) wide.

Most tornadoes have short life spans. Their life spans usually are less than 15 minutes. But some tornadoes last as long as 3 hours.

## The Fujita-Pearson Scale

Since the 1970s, scientists have used the Fujita-Pearson Tornado Intensity Scale to rate the strength of tornadoes. Professor T. Theodore Fujita developed this scale. He was a tornado researcher at the University of Chicago. Allen Pearson also helped develop this scale. Pearson was the director of the

# The Fujita-Pearson Intensity Scale

| | Wind Speeds | Amount of Damage | Type of Damage |
|---|---|---|---|
| **F0** | 0-72 mph<br>0-116 kph | Light Damage | Tree branches broken, trees uprooted, chimneys damaged |
| **F1** | 73-112 mph<br>117-180 kph | Moderate Damage | Surfaces peeled off roofs, mobile homes and cars pushed or overturned |
| **F2** | 113-157 mph<br>182-253 kph | Considerable Damage | Roofs torn off, mobile homes destroyed, large trees uprooted |
| **F3** | 158-206 mph<br>254-332 kph | Severe Damage | Trains overturned, most trees uprooted |
| **F4** | 207-260 mph<br>333-418 kph | Severe Damage | Houses destroyed, cars thrown |
| **F5** | 261-318 mph<br>420-512 kph | Extreme Damage | Bark ripped off trees, cars thrown great distances, strong houses lifted |

National Severe Storm Forecast Center in Kansas City, Missouri.

The Fujita-Pearson scale measures the damage caused by a tornado after the storm has passed. National Weather Service scientists classify a tornado based on its effect on buildings, trees, signs, and other structures. These scientists sometimes view the area from an airplane. This look from above helps them get a better idea of the tornado's path on the ground.

The weakest tornadoes on the Fujita scale have ratings of F0. F0 tornadoes have wind speeds of 72 miles (116 kilometers) per hour or less. F0 tornadoes cause only light damage. The wind from these tornadoes may break tree branches and uproot trees with shallow roots. The wind may damage chimneys and signs.

F1 and F2 tornadoes cause moderate to considerable damage. F1 tornadoes have wind speeds from 73 to 112 miles (117 to 180 kilometers) per hour. F2 tornadoes have wind

speeds from 113 to 157 miles (182 to 253 kilometers) per hour.

F3 and F4 tornadoes cause severe damage. F3 tornadoes have wind speeds from 158 to 206 miles (254 to 332 kilometers) per hour. F4 tornadoes have wind speeds from 207 to 260 miles (333 to 418 kilometers) per hour.

F5 tornadoes have the strongest winds. These tornadoes have winds that range from

261 to 318 miles (420 to 512 kilometers) per hour. F5 tornadoes cause extreme damage. The wind from these tornadoes can rip bark from trees. It can lift houses off their foundations. The wind even can throw cars as far as 109 yards (100 meters).

Nearly 75 percent of all tornadoes are weak F0 and F1 tornadoes. About 25 percent of all tornadoes are strong F2 and F3 tornadoes. Only about 2 percent of all tornadoes reach the F4 and F5 categories. But these tornadoes cause 70 percent of all tornado deaths.

# Chapter 4

# Some Famous Tornadoes

Throughout history, tornadoes have caused much destruction. People study these tornadoes to learn ways to predict storms and to prevent damage.

## The Natchez Tornado

The Natchez Tornado occurred on May 7, 1840. This huge tornado touched ground about 20 miles (32 kilometers) southwest of the town of Natchez, Mississippi. It traveled toward the Mississippi River about 7 miles (11 kilometers) outside of Natchez.

The tornado caused severe destruction on both sides of the river. Riverboats battered

**Tornadoes can destroy a great deal of property.** ⟵

**The Great Tri-State Tornado is considered the most destructive tornado in U.S. history.**

against each other and sank. The tornado also picked up debris as it traveled. The tornado's force tossed these objects into the air. The debris struck people. Many people were injured. Some died as a result of their injuries. About 270 people died on the river that day. Another 50 died in Natchez.

## The Great Tri-State Tornado

The Great Tri-State Tornado is considered the most deadly and most destructive tornado in U.S. history. This storm occurred on the afternoon of March 18, 1925.

The tornado first touched ground near Ellington, Missouri. It then tore through Missouri, Illinois, and Indiana. The tornado lasted more than three hours. Its path was 219 miles (352 kilometers) long and .75 miles (1.2 kilometers) wide. The tornado moved in a straight line during the first three hours.

This tornado was difficult for people to see. The low storm clouds made the sky dark. Dirt and debris were blowing everywhere. The dark skies and the storm's speed gave people little time to react.

The tornado traveled at an average speed of 62 miles (100 kilometers) per hour. Its top speed was 73 miles (117 kilometers) per hour. Today, some scientists believe this storm may have actually been two or more tornadoes traveling close together.

**In April of 1974, the largest outbreak of tornadoes in history took place.**

The Great Tri-State Tornado finally broke apart near Princeton, Indiana. Nearly 700 people died in the storm. More than 2,000 others were injured. The storm destroyed 11,000 homes.

### The Gainesville Tornadoes

Two large tornadoes swept through Gainesville, Georgia, on April 6, 1936. One tornado entered the city from the southwest. The other came in from the west. The tornadoes then met and followed the same path through the city. The tornadoes' path was four blocks wide. Debris as deep as 10 feet (3 meters) filled the streets after the storm.

The Cooper Pants Factory in Gainesville collapsed and caught fire. The fire killed 70 people. Most of these people were young factory workers. This is the largest death toll in a single building caused by a U.S. tornado. The damage was so severe in some areas that it was impossible to tell which people died in which buildings. More than 200 people died and about 1,600 were injured as a result of these tornadoes.

## The Super Outbreak of 1974

Most tornadoes are single storms. But multiple tornadoes sometimes form inside large thunderstorm systems. On April 3 and April 4,

More than 45 people died during the Kansas and
Oklahoma Tornado Outbreak.

1974, the largest outbreak of tornadoes in
history took place.

During an 18-hour period, 148 tornadoes
developed. These tornadoes occurred in 13
states and traveled about 2,500 miles
(4,000 kilometers). Of these tornadoes, 30
were classified as F4 or F5. More than 300
people died and 6,000 people were injured
during these storms.

## Kansas and Oklahoma Outbreak

On May 3, 1999, Tornado Alley residents knew severe weather was on the way. More than 170 tornado warnings were announced on television, radio, weather radios, and the Internet. Community sirens went off. Police drove up and down the streets. They told people to take shelter.

On that day, a total of 96 tornadoes raged across Oklahoma, Kansas, Texas, Nebraska, and South Dakota. The largest number was in Oklahoma. The state had 66 tornadoes that day. Of these tornadoes, 52 were in the Oklahoma City area. One F5 tornado stayed on the ground for nearly 90 minutes. In Kansas, an F4 tornado traveled 17 miles (27 kilometers), hitting the cities of Wichita and Haysville.

Altogether, 47 people died during the tornado outbreak. Most of the deaths were in the Oklahoma City area. Eleven counties were declared disaster areas.

The death toll could have been much higher if warning systems had not been in place. One weather researcher estimated that more than 700 people could have died.

# Chapter 5

# Surviving a Tornado

Much of the destruction caused by tornadoes occurs when people are not prepared for the storms. Early predictions, better warning systems, and increased education help people prepare for tornadoes. This preparation can prevent damage, injuries, and even death.

### Predicting Tornadoes

People first correctly predicted a tornado in 1948. Two officers at the Tinker Air Force Base in Oklahoma City predicted that conditions were right for a tornado to form. Today, the National Weather Service (NWS) issues more than 15,000 severe storm and tornado predictions each year.

Technology makes tornado predictions possible. Satellites orbiting the Earth provide

**Tornadoes can cause a great deal of damage in populated areas.**

**Tornado sirens warn people that a tornado has been spotted.**

scientists with images of global weather patterns. These images show scientists when the weather conditions are right for tornadoes to form. Doppler radar systems provide detailed information about specific storm systems. Computer networks then help scientists process this information quickly. By the late 1990s, people heard tornado warnings an average of 12 minutes before the storms struck.

## Tornado Watches and Warnings

The NWS announces tornado watches and warnings. These announcements tell people that a tornado may be approaching an area. The NWS usually announces watches and warnings on television and radio.

The NWS issues a tornado watch when tornadoes are possible. Watches cover large areas. Watches indicate that conditions are right for tornadoes to form.

The NWS announces a tornado warning when a tornado has been seen by a person. The NWS also issues a warning if radar has detected a tornado. Community sirens are sounded. Tornado warning announcements interrupt television and radio shows.

People cannot rely entirely on warnings. Tornadoes sometimes do not show up on radar. Newly formed tornadoes might not be visible to the human eye. Rain or low clouds might hide tornadoes. Tornadoes also behave unpredictably. They often switch directions or turn in circles. They might lift up and touch ground again in another spot.

## Safety Measures

People must take safety measures during tornado watches and warnings. Flying debris causes most injuries and deaths during tornadoes. People should stay indoors during tornadoes to avoid debris. They should immediately go to storm shelters or basements. People should go to the lowest levels of buildings without basements. Small inner rooms such as bathrooms or closets usually are the safest rooms. People also should stay out of elevators during tornadoes. The power often goes out during storms. People then may be trapped in elevators.

People should keep away from windows and corners. Tornadoes may break windows. Debris may pile up in corners. People should avoid rooms with high ceilings such as auditoriums or gymnasiums. Tornadoes often damage the heavy roofs of these buildings. People also should crouch beneath heavy objects such as tables, workbenches, or staircases. They should cover their heads with their hands.

People who live in mobile homes may be in extreme danger during tornadoes. Strong winds can easily tip or throw mobile homes. People who live in mobile homes should not stay inside during

**Organizations work together to help rebuild communities after tornadoes strike.**

tornadoes. They should go to nearby storm shelters or to other sturdy buildings.

People can get caught outside during storms. People who are outside or in their vehicles should not try to outrun storms. Tornadoes can quickly change directions. They can toss cars or trucks in the air. People should leave their vehicles and find shelter in a nearby building. If this is not possible, people should leave their vehicles. They should lie on the ground in a ditch. They also should cover their head and neck with their arms.

**People still cannot predict tornadoes with complete accuracy.**

People can prepare for storms in other ways. People should know the emergency policies of their schools or work places. These plans tell people where to seek shelter in case of a storm. People may contact their city governments to learn more about local emergency procedures. People should always follow the instructions of local authorities during a tornado.

## After a Tornado

The skies often are clear after a tornado. But

there still can be danger. Damaged buildings may collapse. Live power lines may be on the ground. Trees may topple over unexpectedly. Even the drinking water may be unsafe. Gas leaks and damaged electrical systems may cause fires. These fires can be especially dangerous. Fire trucks may not be able to get to fire sites quickly because of the destruction.

Most communities have disaster plans in place to help residents cope with the effects of tornadoes. Organizations work together after disasters to help rebuild communities. These organizations might include police and rescue units, city engineers, and utility workers. They also may include insurance companies or national groups such as the Red Cross and the National Guard.

Communities may take a long time to recover from a tornado. Buildings need to be repaired or rebuilt. This construction can take months or even years. Trees are difficult to replace. Large trees sometimes take a century or more to grow.

People cannot prevent tornadoes. They cannot even predict these storms with complete accuracy. But warning and preparation measures can help people live to tell about these violent storms.

# Words to Know

**air pressure** (AIR PRESH-ur)—the weight of air on a surface

**condensation** (kon-den-SAY-shuhn)—the act of turning a gas into a liquid

**cumulonimbus cloud** (kyoom-yoo-lo-NIM-bus KLOUD)—a cloud that produces a thunderstorm

**debris** (duh-BREE)—the remains of something that has been destroyed

**downdraft** (DOWN-draft)—a downward movement of air

**evaporation** (ee-vap-uh-RAY-shuhn)—the act of a liquid turning into a gas

**hail** (HAYL)—balls of ice that may fall during thunderstorms

**satellite** (SAT-uh-lite)—a spacecraft that circles around the Earth; satellites often are used to gather and send weather information.

**updraft** (UHP-draft)—an upward movement of air

# To Learn More

**Hopping, Lorraine Jean.** *Wild Weather: Tornadoes!* Hello Reader! Level 4. New York: Scholastic, 1994.

**Kahl, Jonathan D.** *Storm Warning: Tornadoes and Hurricanes.* How's the Weather? Minneapolis: Lerner, 1993.

**Penner, Lucille Recht.** *Twisters!* Step into Reading. New York: Random House, 1996.

**Rose, Sally.** *Tornadoes!* New York: Simon Spotlight, 1999.

# → Useful Addresses

**American Meteorological Society**
45 Beacon Street
Boston, MA  02108-3693

**FEMA (Federal Emergency Management
Agency)**
500 C Street S.W.
Room 824
Washington, DC  20472-0001

**National Weather Service, National Oceanic
and Atmospheric Administration**
1325 East-West Highway
Silver Spring, MD  20910

**The Tornado Project**
P.O. Box 302
St. Johnsbury, VT  05819

# Internet Sites

**How Tornadoes Work**
http://www.howstuffworks.com/tornado.htm

**Tornadoes**
http://www.fema.gov/kids/tornado.htm

**Tornadoes—Nature's Most Violent Storms**
http://www.nws.noaa.gov/om/tornado.htm

**Tornado Project Online**
http://www.tornadoproject.com

**Tornado Warning!**
http://www.discovery.com/area/science/tornado/
    tornado.html

# Index